Fiona MacKay Young

Praise for My Inspirational Journals

What a great idea this Grandmother's Journal is. I am writing it especially to share with my granddaughter when she is older.

Maria Hernandez, Los Angeles, CA

I thought I'd remember all the special moments from my kids' childhood, but I'm sure I have forgotten so much. I'm not about to make that mistake with my grandchildren. It's all going in my Grandmother's journal.

Rachel Godfrey, Newcastle, UK

Photos are great, and so are movies. But to just sit down and read about how you felt as the special moments happened is priceless.

Jan Archibald, Toronto, ON

"Grandmother's Inspirational Quotation Journal"
is in the
"Inspirational Quotation Journal" series.

www.myinspiratationaljournals.com

Keeping you inspired!

Grandmother's
Inspirational Quotation **Journal**

Making Memories

Copyright (c) 2014 by Fiona MacKay Young. All rights reserved.

No part of this publication may be reproduced, or transmitted in any form or by any means, electronic, mechanical, photocopying, recording, scanning or otherwise, except as permitted under International Copyright Laws, without either the prior written permission of the author or authorization through payment of the appropriate per-copy fee.

Requests for permission should be addressed to Fiona MacKay Young at fionamackayyoung@gmail.com.

This publication is designed to provide inspiration and encouragement in regard to the subject matter covered. It is sold with the understanding that the author is not responsible for any reaction to, or action taken or not taken as a result of reading this material.

Copyright (c) 2014 by Fiona MacKay Young.

Grandmother's Inspirational Quotation Journal
Making Memories

Introduction

Do you remember all the special times when your children were small – what they said and did and how you felt about it?

If you did not journal at the time, it is unlikely you do remember it all. Pictures help. Videos are great. But there is nothing like reading how you actually felt at the time or about the look on your child's face at a certain moment.

Now you have the chance all over again - this time with your grandchildren.

Journaling creates a treasure chest which, when opened, brings back these moments so clearly. What cute phrases do your grandchildren use? What words do they use incorrectly that makes you laugh?

You may or may not recall a recording by Helen Reddy of "I am Woman" in the '70s. My then-2½ year old son, not surprisingly unfamiliar with the word "invincible" went around the house singing "I am strong, I am a

Grandmother's Inspirational Quotation Journal
Making Memories

vegetable". (The correct line, of course, being "I am strong, I am invincible, I am woman.")

I remember that one and I remember many more – but I know I have forgotten so many precious moments that could have been memories today if only I would have journaled about them.

You do not have to journal every day, or at any specific interval. Just wait till something special happens and jot it down.

If you feel like it, you can write it out in detail, but if not, just a few words to remind you of that time will still bring the memories flooding back at a later date.

Your Grandmother's Journal can be just for you.

Or it can be something you go over with your grandchildren when they are older.

Or it can be a wonderful gift to your son or daughter, who probably is too busy dealing with their family to have time to journal regularly.

Grandmother's Inspirational Quotation Journal
Making Memories

The other thing journaling about your grandchildren can do, is that it can bring back hitherto forgotten memories of your own children's early years, especially when a grandchild turns out to be very like his or her parent.

It takes very little time but is a priceless investment.

Journaling in general is an extremely healthy activity.

It allows you to express yourself, to "get things out".

It saves you from trying to remember things (which gets harder as we get older) and help you focus on the important things in life.

Focused journaling, which is journaling on a specific topic, (in this case grand parenting) help you focus on your grandchildren and the joys of being a grandparent.

It is a well-known fact that what you focus on expands so by focusing on your role as grandparent you become more centered in it, and can become a stronger influence for good in the life of your grandchildren.

Grandmother's Inspirational Quotation Journal
Making Memories

If you have problems or misunderstandings, they too can be helped by journaling as it gives you a clearer view of the situation, which it turn makes it easier to decide what best to do next.

And lastly – it is fun!

Just to sit down and write out the joys of being a grandparent is just pure fun!

So enjoy.

Write to your heart's content.

Stick in the appropriate journal entries drawings from your grandchildren, homemade cards etc.

This book can become a treasure to you and to your family – if only you give it a chance by writing down a few notes about your grand parenting days as they happen.

Happy grand parenting.

Grandmother's Inspirational Quotation Journal
Making Memories

Grandmother's Inspirational Quotation Journal
Making Memories

Grandmother's Inspirational Quotation Journal
Making Memories

Grandmother's Inspirational Quotation Journal
Making Memories

Grandmother's Inspirational Quotation Journal
Making Memories

Start Journaling here....

Grandmother's Inspirational Quotation Journal
Making Memories

Perfect love sometimes does not come until the first grandchild.

Welsh Proverb

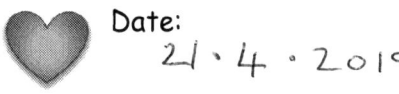

Date: 21.4.2019

My grandchildren are
    Samuel Arelio - born 22.4.2016
Always Loved.   died 6.5.2016
    Isaac David born 9.10.2017
    Alice Rose   born 18.1.2018

Today is Easter Sunday and I am staying with my dad. We have hosted a family lunch. Instead of Easter Eggs we gave Isaac & Alice their first Duplo sets. I hope they enjoy them as much

Grandmother's Inspirational Quotation Journal
Making Memories

A house needs a grandma in it.

Louisa May Alcott

 Date:

as Philip & Helen did. Isaac says a lot of words including "Grandma" & Grandad! Alice is becoming more sociable, with a lovely smile. Both are walking and never stop.

Becoming a grandmother is wonderful. One moment you're just a mother. The next you are all-wise and prehistoric.

Pam Brown

Date:

How many Hugs do you rate your day:
1 Hug   2 Hugs   3 Hugs   4 Hugs   5 Hugs

Grandmother's Inspirational Quotation Journal
Making Memories

Grandchildren are God's way of compensating us for growing old.

Mary H. Waldrip

Date:

How many Hugs do you rate your day:
1 Hug   2 Hugs   3 Hugs   4 Hugs   5 Hugs

Grandmother's Inspirational Quotation Journal
Making Memories

If nothing is going well, call your grandmother.

Italian Proverb

Date:

How many Hugs do you rate your day:
1 Hug   2 Hugs   3 Hugs   4 Hugs   5 Hugs

Grandmother — a wonderful mother with lots of practice.

Unknown

Date:

How many Hugs do you rate your day:
1 Hug 2 Hugs 3 Hugs 4 Hugs 5 Hugs

Grandmother's Inspirational Quotation Journal
Making Memories

Grandparents make the world a little softer, a little kinder, a little warmer.

Unknown

Date:

How many Hugs do you rate your day:
1 Hug 2 Hugs 3 Hugs 4 Hugs 5 Hugs

Grandmother's Inspirational Quotation Journal
Making Memories

I like to do nice things for my grandchildren — like buy them those toys I've always wanted to play with.

Gene Perret

Studies have shown that 100% of all Grandchildren are gifted.

Unknown

Date:

How many Hugs do you rate your day:
1 Hug   2 Hugs   3 Hugs   4 Hugs   5 Hugs

Date:

How many Hugs do you rate your day:
1 Hug   2 Hugs   3 Hugs   4 Hugs   5 Hugs

Grandmother's Inspirational Quotation Journal
Making Memories

Grandma and Grandpa tell me a story and snuggle me with your love.
When I'm in your arms, the world seems small and we're blessed by the heavens above.

Laura Spiess

Date:

How many Hugs do you rate your day:
1 Hug   2 Hugs   3 Hugs   4 Hugs   5 Hugs

If your baby is "beautiful and perfect, never cries or fusses, sleeps on schedule and burps on demand, an angel all the time," you're the grandma.

Teresa Bloomingdale

Date:

How many Hugs do you rate your day:
1 Hug   2 Hugs   3 Hugs   4 Hugs   5 Hugs

Grandmother's Inspirational Quotation Journal
Making Memories

Every grandparent knows that winning a child's heart is as easy as ABC:
Always
Bring
Candy.

Unknown

Date:

How many Hugs do you rate your day:
1 Hug 2 Hugs 3 Hugs 4 Hugs 5 Hugs

Grandmother's Inspirational Quotation Journal
Making Memories

Grandchildren are the gifts of yesterday, the pride of today and the joy of tomorrow.

Unknown

Date:

How many Hugs do you rate your day:
1 Hug   2 Hugs   3 Hugs   4 Hugs   5 Hugs

Grandmother's Inspirational Quotation Journal
Making Memories

Let's eat Grandma.

Let's eat, Grandma.

Punctuation Saves Lives!

Unknown

Date:

How many Hugs do you rate your day:
1 Hug   2 Hugs   3 Hugs   4 Hugs   5 Hugs

Grandmother's Inspirational Quotation Journal
Making Memories

Grandmas are moms with lots of frosting.

Unknown

Date:

How many Hugs do you rate your day:
1 Hug 2 Hugs 3 Hugs 4 Hugs 5 Hugs

What children need most are the essentials that grandparents provide in abundance. They give unconditional love, kindness, patience, humor, comfort, lessons in life. And, most importantly, cookies.

Rudy Giuliani

Date:

How many Hugs do you rate your day:
1 Hug   2 Hugs   3 Hugs   4 Hugs   5 Hugs

Grandmother's Inspirational Quotation Journal
Making Memories

Grandmas never run out of hugs or cookies.

Unknown

Date:

How many Hugs do you rate your day:
1 Hug   2 Hugs   3 Hugs   4 Hugs   5 Hugs

Do you know why grandchildren are always so full of energy? They suck it out of their grandparents.

Gene Perret

Date:

How many Hugs do you rate your day:
1 Hug 2 Hugs 3 Hugs 4 Hugs 5 Hugs

Grandmother's Inspirational Quotation Journal
Making Memories

The simplest toy, one which even the youngest child can operate, is called a grandparent.

Sam Levenson

Date:

How many Hugs do you rate your day:
1 Hug   2 Hugs   3 Hugs   4 Hugs   5 Hugs

Grandmother's Inspirational Quotation Journal
Making Memories

A grandmother pretends she doesn't know who you are on Halloween.

Erma Bombeck

Date:

How many Hugs do you rate your day:
1 Hug   2 Hugs   3 Hugs   4 Hugs   5 Hugs

Grandmother's Inspirational Quotation Journal
Making Memories

One of life's greatest mysteries is how the boy who wasn't good enough to marry your daughter can be the father of the smartest grandchild in the world.

Jewish proverb

Date:

How many Hugs do you rate your day:
1 Hug   2 Hugs   3 Hugs   4 Hugs   5 Hugs

Only your grandpa and your grandma can be relied on never to get angry with you, even when you've been really, really naughty

Unknown

Date:

How many Hugs do you rate your day:
1 Hug   2 Hugs   3 Hugs   4 Hugs   5 Hugs

Grandmother's Inspirational Quotation Journal
Making Memories

To be able to watch your children's children grow up is truly a blessing from above.

Byron Pulsifer

Date:

How many Hugs do you rate your day:
1 Hug   2 Hugs   3 Hugs   4 Hugs   5 Hugs

Grandmother-grandchild relationships are simple. Grandmas are short on criticism and long on love.

Unknown

Date:

How many Hugs do you rate your day:
1 Hug   2 Hugs   3 Hugs   4 Hugs   5 Hugs

Grandmother's Inspirational Quotation Journal
Making Memories

What Are Grandmas For?

Grandmas are for stories
about things of long ago.
Grandmas are for caring
about all the things you know...
Grandmas are for rocking you
and singing you to sleep,
Grandmas are for giving you
nice memories to keep...
Grandmas are for knowing
all the things you're dreaming of
But, most importantly of all,
grandmas are for love.

Unknown

Date:

How many Hugs do you rate your day:
1 Hug   2 Hugs   3 Hugs   4 Hugs   5 Hugs

You can't scare me.
I have grandchildren.

Unknown

Date:

How many Hugs do you rate your day:
1 Hug   2 Hugs   3 Hugs   4 Hugs   5 Hugs

Grandmother's Inspirational Quotation Journal
Making Memories

When God made my grandchildren He was just showing off

Unknown

Date:

How many Hugs do you rate your day:
1 Hug 2 Hugs 3 Hugs 4 Hugs 5 Hugs

Grandmother's Inspirational Quotation Journal
Making Memories

I didn't do it.
Nobody saw me do it.
I want my Grandma.

Unknown

Date:

How many Hugs do you rate your day:
1 Hug 2 Hugs 3 Hugs 4 Hugs 5 Hugs

Grandmother's Inspirational Quotation Journal
Making Memories

What a bargain grandchildren are! I give them my loose change, and they give me a million dollars' worth of pleasure.

Gene Perret

Date:

How many Hugs do you rate your day:
1 Hug   2 Hugs   3 Hugs   4 Hugs   5 Hugs

Our grandchildren accept us for ourselves, without rebuke or effort to change us, as no one in our entire lives has ever done, not our parents, siblings, spouses, friends - and hardly ever our own grown children.

Ruth Goode

Date:

How many Hugs do you rate your day:
1 Hug   2 Hugs   3 Hugs   4 Hugs   5 Hugs

Grandmother's Inspirational Quotation Journal
Making Memories

My grandmother started walking five miles a day when she was sixty. She's ninety-seven now, and we don't know where on earth she is.

Ellen DeGeneres

Date:

How many Hugs do you rate your day:
1 Hug   2 Hugs   3 Hugs   4 Hugs   5 Hugs

Grandmother's Inspirational Quotation Journal
Making Memories

Few things are more delightful than grandchildren fighting over your lap.

Doug Larson

Date:

How many Hugs do you rate your day:
1 Hug 2 Hugs 3 Hugs 4 Hugs 5 Hugs

It's amazing how grandparents seem so young once you become one.

Unknown

Date:

How many Hugs do you rate your day:
1 Hug   2 Hugs   3 Hugs   4 Hugs   5 Hugs

Grandmother's Inspirational Quotation Journal
Making Memories

If nothing is going well, call your grandmother.

Italian proverb

Date:

How many Hugs do you rate your day:
1 Hug   2 Hugs   3 Hugs   4 Hugs   5 Hugs

My grandson was visiting one day when he asked, 'Gramma, do you know how you and God are alike?' I mentally polished my halo while I asked, 'No, how are we alike?' 'You're both old,' he replied."

Unknown

Date:

How many Hugs do you rate your day:
1 Hug   2 Hugs   3 Hugs   4 Hugs   5 Hugs

Grandmothers are the people who take delight
in hearing babies breathing into the telephone.

Unknown

Date:

How many Hugs do you rate your day:
1 Hug   2 Hugs   3 Hugs   4 Hugs   5 Hugs

Grandmother's Inspirational Quotation Journal
Making Memories

Being pretty on the inside means you don't hit your brother and you eat all your peas - that's what my grandma taught me.

Lord Chesterfield

Date:

How many Hugs do you rate your day:
1 Hug   2 Hugs   3 Hugs   4 Hugs   5 Hugs

I thought I had my life organized - and then I became a grandma.

Unknown

Date:

How many Hugs do you rate your day:
1 Hug   2 Hugs   3 Hugs   4 Hugs   5 Hugs

Grandmother's Inspirational Quotation Journal
Making Memories

The world needs grandmas and grandpas - those grandkids aren't going to spoil themselves.

Unknown

Date:

How many Hugs do you rate your day:
1 Hug   2 Hugs   3 Hugs   4 Hugs   5 Hugs

We may not be rich and famous, but our grandchildren are priceless

Unknown

Date:

How many Hugs do you rate your day:
1 Hug   2 Hugs   3 Hugs   4 Hugs   5 Hugs

Grandmothers are just antique little girls.

Unknown

Date:

How many Hugs do you rate your day:
1 Hug   2 Hugs   3 Hugs   4 Hugs   5 Hugs

Grandmother's Inspirational Quotation Journal
Making Memories

We should all have one person
who knows how to bless us
despite the evidence;
Grandmother was that person
to me.

Phyllis Theroux

Date:

How many Hugs do you rate your day:
1 Hug   2 Hugs   3 Hugs   4 Hugs   5 Hugs

Grandmother's Inspirational Quotation Journal
Making Memories

If becoming a grandmother was only a matter of choice, I should advise every one of you straight away to become one. There is no fun for old people like it!

Hannah Whithall Smith

Date:

How many Hugs do you rate your day:
1 Hug   2 Hugs   3 Hugs   4 Hugs   5 Hugs

Grandmother's Inspirational Quotation Journal
Making Memories

Nobody can do for little children what grandparents do. Grandparents sort of sprinkle stardust over the lives of little children.

Alex Haley

Date:

How many Hugs do you rate your day:
1 Hug   2 Hugs   3 Hugs   4 Hugs   5 Hugs

Grandmother's Inspirational Quotation Journal
Making Memories

Something magical happens when parents turns into grandparents. Their attitude changes from "money-doesn't-grow-on-trees" to spending it like it does.

Paul Linden

Date:

How many Hugs do you rate your day:
1 Hug   2 Hugs   3 Hugs   4 Hugs   5 Hugs

Grandmother's Inspirational Quotation Journal
Making Memories

All Grandmothers like letters. Even if they just consist of a squiggle and a dirty finger mark.

Unknown

Date:

How many Hugs do you rate your day:
1 Hug   2 Hugs   3 Hugs   4 Hugs   5 Hugs

Grandmother's Inspirational Quotation Journal
Making Memories

No cowboy was ever faster on the draw than a grandmother pulling a baby picture out of a wallet.

Unknown

Date:

How many Hugs do you rate your day:
1 Hug   2 Hugs   3 Hugs   4 Hugs   5 Hugs

Grandmother's Inspirational Quotation Journal
Making Memories

To show a child what has once delighted you, to find the child's delight added to your own, so that there is now a double delight seen in the glow of trust and affection, this is happiness.

J.B. Priestley

Date:

How many Hugs do you rate your day:
1 Hug   2 Hugs   3 Hugs   4 Hugs   5 Hugs

Can I put "being a grandparent" on my resume?

Unknown

Date:

How many Hugs do you rate your day:
1 Hug   2 Hugs   3 Hugs   4 Hugs   5 Hugs

Grandmother's Inspirational Quotation Journal
Making Memories

Mommy knows a lot, but
Grandma knows everything

Unknown

Date:

How many Hugs do you rate your day:
1 Hug   2 Hugs   3 Hugs   4 Hugs   5 Hugs

Grandmother's Inspirational Quotation Journal
Making Memories

Hugs were invented to let grandkids know you love them without having to say anything.

Unknown

Date:

How many Hugs do you rate your day:
1 Hug   2 Hugs   3 Hugs   4 Hugs   5 Hugs

Grandmother's Inspirational Quotation Journal
Making Memories

Grandchildren don't stay young forever, which is good because Pop-pops have only so many horsey rides in them.

Gene Perret

Date:

How many Hugs do you rate your day:
1 Hug   2 Hugs   3 Hugs   4 Hugs   5 Hugs

Grandmother's Inspirational Quotation Journal
Making Memories

Elephants and grandchildren never forget.

Andy Rooney

Date:

How many Hugs do you rate your day:
1 Hug   2 Hugs   3 Hugs   4 Hugs   5 Hugs

On the seventh day God rested.
His grandchildren must have
been out of town.

Gene Perret

Date:

How many Hugs do you rate your day:
1 Hug   2 Hugs   3 Hugs   4 Hugs   5 Hugs

Grandmother's Inspirational Quotation Journal
Making Memories

God gave us loving grandchildren as a reward for all our random acts of kindness.

Janet Lanese

Date:

How many Hugs do you rate your day:
1 Hug   2 Hugs   3 Hugs   4 Hugs   5 Hugs

Grandmother's Inspirational Quotation Journal
Making Memories

The handwriting on the wall means the grandchildren found the crayons.

Unknown

Date:

How many Hugs do you rate your day:
1 Hug   2 Hugs   3 Hugs   4 Hugs   5 Hugs

Grandmother's Inspirational Quotation Journal
Making Memories

Just about the time a woman thinks her work is done, she becomes a grandmother.

Edward H. Dreschnack

Date:

How many Hugs do you rate your day:
1 Hug   2 Hugs   3 Hugs   4 Hugs   5 Hugs

Grandmother's Inspirational Quotation Journal
Making Memories

Who needs a fairy godmother when they have a grandma?

Unknown

Date:

How many Hugs do you rate your day:
1 Hug   2 Hugs   3 Hugs   4 Hugs   5 Hugs

Grandkids welcome anytime.
Parents by appointment only.

Unknown

Date:

How many Hugs do you rate your day:
1 Hug   2 Hugs   3 Hugs   4 Hugs   5 Hugs

Grandmother's Inspirational Quotation Journal
Making Memories

Little feet make the biggest footprints in our hearts

Unknown

Date:

How many Hugs do you rate your day:
1 Hug   2 Hugs   3 Hugs   4 Hugs   5 Hugs

Grandmother's Inspirational Quotation Journal
Making Memories

Grandparents are parents, but with more sleep, fewer rules, and an endless supply of cookies.

Unknown

Date:

How many Hugs do you rate your day:
1 Hug   2 Hugs   3 Hugs   4 Hugs   5 Hugs

Grandmother's Inspirational Quotation Journal
Making Memories

If I had known how wonderful it would be to have grandchildren, I'd have had them first.

Lois Wyse

Date:

How many Hugs do you rate your day:
1 Hug   2 Hugs   3 Hugs   4 Hugs   5 Hugs

Grandmother's Inspirational Quotation Journal
Making Memories

Grandparenting:

the ultimate extreme sport

Unknown

Date:

How many Hugs do you rate your day:
1 Hug   2 Hugs   3 Hugs   4 Hugs   5 Hugs

Grandmother's Inspirational Quotation Journal
Making Memories

Unconditional positive regard is rarely given by anyone except a grandparent.

Unknown

Date:

How many Hugs do you rate your day:
1 Hug   2 Hugs   3 Hugs   4 Hugs   5 Hugs

Grandmother's Inspirational Quotation Journal
Making Memories

Slow! Grandparents at Play

Unknown

Date:

How many Hugs do you rate your day:
1 Hug   2 Hugs   3 Hugs   4 Hugs   5 Hugs

No matter how grown up you are, when your two year old grandchild hands you a toy phone, you answer it.

Unknown

Date:

How many Hugs do you rate your day:
1 Hug   2 Hugs   3 Hugs   4 Hugs   5 Hugs

Grandmother's Inspirational Quotation Journal
Making Memories

Sometimes the smallest things take up the most room in our hearts.

AA Milne

Date:

How many Hugs do you rate your day:
1 Hug   2 Hugs   3 Hugs   4 Hugs   5 Hugs

Grandmother's Inspirational Quotation Journal
Making Memories

Please excuse the mess.

My grandkids are making memories

Unknown

Date:

How many Hugs do you rate your day:
1 Hug   2 Hugs   3 Hugs   4 Hugs   5 Hugs

Grandmother's Inspirational Quotation Journal
Making Memories

Grandparents, so easy to operate, even a child can do it.

Unknown

Date:

How many Hugs do you rate your day:
1 Hug   2 Hugs   3 Hugs   4 Hugs   5 Hugs

Grandmother's Inspirational Quotation Journal
Making Memories

A grandmother is someone with silver in her hair and gold in her heart.

Unknown

Date:

How many Hugs do you rate your day:
1 Hug   2 Hugs   3 Hugs   4 Hugs   5 Hugs

Grandmother's Inspirational Quotation Journal
Making Memories

My grandkids believe I'm the oldest thing in the world.

And after two or three hours with them, I believe it, too.

Gene Perret

Date:

How many Hugs do you rate your day:
1 Hug   2 Hugs   3 Hugs   4 Hugs   5 Hugs

Grandmother's Inspirational Quotation Journal
Making Memories

The idea that no one is perfect is a view most commonly held by people with no grandchildren.

Doug Larson

Date:

How many Hugs do you rate your day:
1 Hug   2 Hugs   3 Hugs   4 Hugs   5 Hugs

Grandmother's Inspirational Quotation Journal
Making Memories

To a small child, the perfect granddad is unafraid of big dogs and fierce storms but absolutely terrified of the word "boo."

Robert Brault

Date:

How many Hugs do you rate your day:
1 Hug   2 Hugs   3 Hugs   4 Hugs   5 Hugs

Grandmother's Inspirational Quotation Journal
Making Memories

"You're more trouble than the children are" is the greatest compliment a grandparent can receive.

Gene Perret

Date:

How many Hugs do you rate your day:
1 Hug   2 Hugs   3 Hugs   4 Hugs   5 Hugs

Grandmother's Inspirational Quotation Journal
Making Memories

Grandmother's Inspirational Quotation Journal
Making Memories

Handy
Memory Jogger
Index

Grandmother's Inspirational Quotation Journal
Making Memories

Handy Memory Jogger Index

Date/Page   Quote ☐   Journal Entry ☐
Notes:

Date/Page   Quote ☐   Journal Entry ☐
Notes:

Date/Page   Quote ☐   Journal Entry ☐
Notes:

Date/Page   Quote ☐   Journal Entry ☐
Notes:

Date/Page   Quote ☐   Journal Entry ☐
Notes:

Date/Page   Quote ☐   Journal Entry ☐
Notes:

Date/Page   Quote ☐   Journal Entry ☐
Notes:

Date/Page   Quote ☐   Journal Entry ☐
Notes:

Date/Page   Quote ☐   Journal Entry ☐
Notes:

Grandmother's Inspirational Quotation Journal
Making Memories

Date/Page　　　　Quote ☐　Journal Entry ☐
Notes:

Date/Page　　　　Quote ☐　Journal Entry ☐
Notes:

Date/Page　　　　Quote ☐　Journal Entry ☐
Notes:

Date/Page　　　　Quote ☐　Journal Entry ☐
Notes:

Date/Page　　　　Quote ☐　Journal Entry ☐
Notes:

Date/Page　　　　Quote ☐　Journal Entry ☐
Notes:

Date/Page　　　　Quote ☐　Journal Entry ☐
Notes:

Date/Page　　　　Quote ☐　Journal Entry ☐
Notes:

Date/Page　　　　Quote ☐　Journal Entry ☐
Notes:

Date/Page　　　　Quote ☐　Journal Entry ☐
Notes:

Grandmother's Inspirational Quotation Journal
Making Memories

Date/Page   Quote ☐   Journal Entry ☐
Notes:

Date/Page   Quote ☐   Journal Entry ☐
Notes:

Date/Page   Quote ☐   Journal Entry ☐
Notes:

Date/Page   Quote ☐   Journal Entry ☐
Notes:

Date/Page   Quote ☐   Journal Entry ☐
Notes:

Date/Page   Quote ☐   Journal Entry ☐
Notes:

Date/Page   Quote ☐   Journal Entry ☐
Notes:

Date/Page   Quote ☐   Journal Entry ☐
Notes:

Date/Page   Quote ☐   Journal Entry ☐
Notes:

Date/Page   Quote ☐   Journal Entry ☐
Notes:

Grandmother's Inspirational Quotation Journal
Making Memories

Date/Page   Quote ☐   Journal Entry ☐
Notes:

Date/Page   Quote ☐   Journal Entry ☐
Notes:

Date/Page   Quote ☐   Journal Entry ☐
Notes:

Date/Page   Quote ☐   Journal Entry ☐
Notes:

Date/Page   Quote ☐   Journal Entry ☐
Notes:

Date/Page   Quote ☐   Journal Entry ☐
Notes:

Date/Page   Quote ☐   Journal Entry ☐
Notes:

Date/Page   Quote ☐   Journal Entry ☐
Notes:

Date/Page   Quote ☐   Journal Entry ☐
Notes:

Date/Page   Quote ☐   Journal Entry ☐
Notes:

Grandmother's Inspirational Quotation Journal
Making Memories

Date/Page　　　　　Quote ☐　　Journal Entry ☐
Notes:

Date/Page　　　　　Quote ☐　　Journal Entry ☐
Notes:

Date/Page　　　　　Quote ☐　　Journal Entry ☐
Notes:

Date/Page　　　　　Quote ☐　　Journal Entry ☐
Notes:

Date/Page　　　　　Quote ☐　　Journal Entry ☐
Notes:

Date/Page　　　　　Quote ☐　　Journal Entry ☐
Notes:

Date/Page　　　　　Quote ☐　　Journal Entry ☐
Notes:

Date/Page　　　　　Quote ☐　　Journal Entry ☐
Notes:

Date/Page　　　　　Quote ☐　　Journal Entry ☐
Notes:

Date/Page　　　　　Quote ☐　　Journal Entry ☐
Notes:

Grandmother's Inspirational Quotation Journal
Making Memories

Date/Page   Quote ☐   Journal Entry ☐
Notes:

Date/Page   Quote ☐   Journal Entry ☐
Notes:

Date/Page   Quote ☐   Journal Entry ☐
Notes:

Date/Page   Quote ☐   Journal Entry ☐
Notes:

Date/Page   Quote ☐   Journal Entry ☐
Notes:

Date/Page   Quote ☐   Journal Entry ☐
Notes:

Date/Page   Quote ☐   Journal Entry ☐
Notes:

Date/Page   Quote ☐   Journal Entry ☐
Notes:

Date/Page   Quote ☐   Journal Entry ☐
Notes:

Date/Page   Quote ☐   Journal Entry ☐
Notes:

Grandmother's Inspirational Quotation Journal
Making Memories

Date/Page   Quote ☐   Journal Entry ☐
Notes:

Date/Page   Quote ☐   Journal Entry ☐
Notes:

Date/Page   Quote ☐   Journal Entry ☐
Notes:

Date/Page   Quote ☐   Journal Entry ☐
Notes:

Date/Page   Quote ☐   Journal Entry ☐
Notes:

Date/Page   Quote ☐   Journal Entry ☐
Notes:

Date/Page   Quote ☐   Journal Entry ☐
Notes:

Date/Page   Quote ☐   Journal Entry ☐
Notes:

Date/Page   Quote ☐   Journal Entry ☐
Notes:

Date/Page   Quote ☐   Journal Entry ☐
Notes:

Grandmother's Inspirational Quotation Journal
Making Memories

Date/Page   Quote ☐   Journal Entry ☐
Notes:

Date/Page   Quote ☐   Journal Entry ☐
Notes:

Date/Page   Quote ☐   Journal Entry ☐
Notes:

Date/Page   Quote ☐   Journal Entry ☐
Notes:

Date/Page   Quote ☐   Journal Entry ☐
Notes:

Date/Page   Quote ☐   Journal Entry ☐
Notes:

Date/Page   Quote ☐   Journal Entry ☐
Notes:

Date/Page   Quote ☐   Journal Entry ☐
Notes:

Date/Page   Quote ☐   Journal Entry ☐
Notes:

Date/Page   Quote ☐   Journal Entry ☐
Notes:

Grandmother's Inspirational Quotation Journal
Making Memories

About the Author:

Fiona MacKay Young is a Life Design/ Personal Development coach who uses the tool of journaling both with clients and for herself.

She has journaled for most of her life, and found it extremely helpful as a tool for motivation, creativity and generally keeping her life on an even keel.

She has developed her Inspirational Journals to help others maximize on the benefits of writing from the heart on a regular basis. Fiona totally believes that this is a tool to improve life, better relationships and generally enjoy all that life has to offer.

Susan spends her time between the Pacific West Coast and various parts of the British Isles.

You can contact Fiona at
fionamackayyoung@gmail.com

Grandmother's Inspirational Quotation Journal
Making Memories

Printed in Great Britain
by Amazon